AUDIO ACCESS INCLUDED

PLAYBACK+
• *Pitch • Balance • Loop*

ALTO SAX

Billie Eilish

Audio arrangements by Peter Deneff

To access audio, visit:
www.halleonard.com/mylibrary

"Enter Code"
6675-3333-1353-5187

ISBN 978-1-5400-9209-0

HAL•LEONARD®

Visit Hal Leonard Online at
www.halleonard.com

Contact us:
Hal Leonard
7777 West Bluemound Road
Milwaukee, WI 53213
Email: info@halleonard.com

In Europe, contact:
Hal Leonard Europe Limited
42 Wigmore Street
Marylebone, London, W1U 2RN
Email: info@halleonardeurope.com

In Australia, contact:
Hal Leonard Australia Pty. Ltd.
4 Lentara Court
Cheltenham, Victoria, 3192 Australia
Email: info@halleonard.com.au

CONTENTS

BAD GUY

ALTO SAX

Words and Music by BILLIE EILISH O'CONNEL
and FINNEAS O'CONNEL

I LOVE YOU

LTO SAX

Words and Music by BILLIE EILISH O'CONNELL
and FINNEAS O'CONNELL

EVERYTHING I WANTED

ALTO SAX

Words and Music by BILLIE EILISH O'CONNEL
and FINNEAS O'CONNEL

Idontwannabeyouanymore

ALTO SAX

Words and Music by BILLIE EILISH O'CONNELL
and FINNEAS O'CONNELL

LOVELY

ALTO SAX

Words and Music by BILLIE EILISH O'CONNELL,
FINNEAS O'CONNELL and KHALID ROBINSON

NO TIME TO DIE

ALTO SAX

Words and Music by BILLIE EILISH O'CONNELL
and FINNEAS O'CONNELL

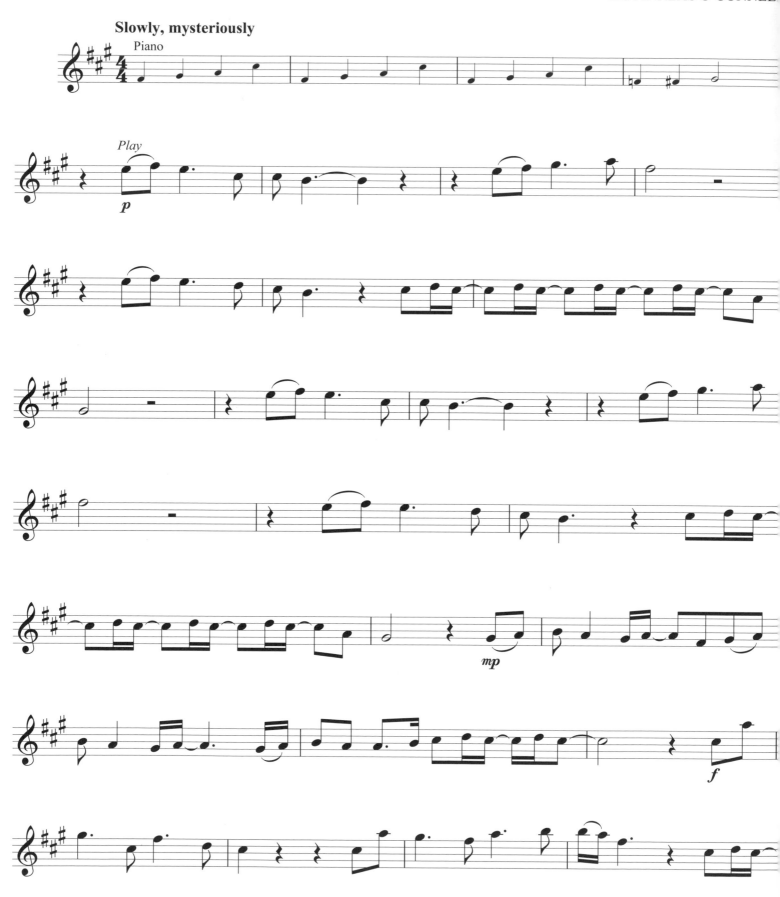

OCEAN EYES

ALTO SAX

Words and Music by
FINNEAS O'CONNELL

YOU SHOULD SEE ME IN A CROWN

ALTO SAX

Words and Music by BILLIE EILISH O'CONNELL
and FINNEAS O'CONNELL

WHEN THE PARTY'S OVER

ALTO SAX

Words and Music by
FINNEAS O'CONNELL